Volume 116 of the Yale Series of Younger Poets

Mothman Apologia

ROBERT WOOD LYNN

Foreword by

RAE ARMANTROUT

Yale

UNIVERSITY PRESS

New Haven and London

PUBLISHED WITH ASSISTANCE FROM
A GRANT TO HONOR JAMES MERRILL.

Yale University Press books may be purchased in quantity for educational,
business, or promotional use. For information, please e-mail sales.
press@yale.edu (U.S. office) or sales@yaleup.co.uk (U.K. office).

Designed by Dustin Kilgore.
Set in Yale New & Yale Display type by Motto Publishing Services.
Printed in the United States of America.

Library of Congress Control Number: 2021946536
ISBN 978-0-300-26108-0 (hardcover : alk. paper)
ISBN 978-0-300-26107-3 (paperback : alk. paper)

A catalogue record for this book is available from the British Library.

This paper meets the requirements of
ANSI/NISO Z39.48-1992 (Permanence of Paper).

10 9 8 7 6 5 4 3 2

for A. C. and C. W.
who are not here to read this

"

It is so American, fire. So like us.
Its desolation. And its eventual, brief triumph.

"

—Larry Levis
from "My Story in a Late Style of Fire"

Contents

Foreword by Rae Armantrout xi

(The Mothman Gets High) 1

PART I

    (The Mothman Googles Its Own Name) 5

    First of Ten Elegies for Fire and Oxycodone 7

    Second of Ten Elegies for Fire and Oxycodone. 9

    (The Mothman at Twelve) 11

    Psalm for the Haters in the Back 13

    Voicemail from My Mother. 15

    (The Mothman Pronounces Appalachia) 17

    Third of Ten Elegies for Fire and Oxycodone. 19

    Fourth of Ten Elegies for Fire and Oxycodone 21

    (The Mothman at the Psychiatrist's Office in the City) 23

    It Was Time Again for Bushhogging the Paddock 25

    Prayer for the Shitstains. 27

    (The Mothman Watches a TV Movie and Resolves
        to Steal the Declaration of Independence) 29

    I Never Knew What They Meant by Flyover Country. 31

    The Best Shot in the House. 33

PART II

    (The Mothman Leaves the Used Car Lot Empty-Handed) 37

    The Season We Danced Alone While Pumping Gas 39

    Walking Blues Not Packaged for Individual Sale 41

    (The Mothman Picks Up a Misdemeanor) 43

    Fifth of Ten Elegies for Fire and Oxycodone 45

    Sixth of Ten Elegies for Fire and Oxycodone 47

    (The Mothman Dabbles in Etymology) 49

    Coming To. 51

    I Remember You Best as the Man 53

    (The Mothman Might Oughta Go Home) 55

    Augury 57

    About the Phones 59

PART III

    (The Mothman on the Bullshit Curse of Interesting Times) 63

    Seventh of Ten Elegies for Fire and Oxycodone 65

    Eighth of Ten Elegies for Fire and Oxycodone 67

    (The Mothman Startles the Neighbors) 69

    Extraction 71

    The Summer After the Winter I Taught You How to Start a Fire 73

    (The Mothman Reads from *The Book of the Dead*) 75

    Ninth of Ten Elegies for Fire and Oxycodone 77

    Tenth of Ten Elegies for Fire and Oxycodone. 79

    (The Mothman Drops Out) 81

    Peepers in February. 83

    Sneaking onto the Reservoir Again 85

    (The Mothman Looks Back). 87

    Let the Child Think She's Found an Arrowhead. 89

    A Pangram for the Post-Modern Typefaces 91

    Eleventh of Ten Elegies for Fire and Oxycodone. 93

    (The Mothman Gets Clean) 95

Notes 97

Acknowledgments. 101

Foreword

Mothman Apologia got my attention on the first page when I read, "I've never felt further from another than when ". . . trying to point out a star." I've had this experience but it's not something I've ever seen depicted in a poem. Getting another person to share your (literal) perspective isn't easy.

This book was surprising phrase to phrase as well as in its overall form. The speaker, I could really say the narrator, is sometimes a teenage boy in the mountains of Virginia, sometimes a local apparition known as The Mothman (more on that later). These speakers create an entwined elegy for a dead friend and for a region devastated by oxycodone and extractive industries. It's also an allegory (complete with a canny tip of the hat to Dante) which places the Sackler Bros. and Purdue Pharma in a place that, if not exactly hell, is close enough.

"Tenth of Ten Elegies for Fire and Oxycodone" begins with what I assume is a legal doctrine: "The law of causation   has a special doctrine   *the two fires rule*   preserves/responsibility for damage done   by multiple causes   each sufficient to cause/the whole harm   say two guys start   two different fires . . . behind your house . . . when called to court   each arsonist paints the other/as the whole damn cause . . . say three brothers start a company   in the woods behind your life." This book is Robert Wood Lynn's answer to what happens next. It confronts a systemic neglect. In "I Never Knew What They Meant by Flyover Country" the speaker comes to understand the term when he takes his first plane ride: "Our fields stretched out/endless in orderly blanks, redactions . . ."

The causes of the area's devastation are multiple. In "Psychiatrist's Office in the City" the Mothman tells a doctor that "there are whole parts of West/Virginia named after explosives which is where they saw the first of us moth-people." You could describe the titular Mothman is as a symbol of the way this region is disrespected and disregarded: ". . . knock a lid open and out of all these/mineshafts climb monsters . . ."

Lynn can write sentences like zingers, so pithy it takes a moment to register them; for instance, "*Appalachia* doesn't/rhyme with *euthanasia* any more than *Eurydice* rhymes with/*cowardice*." Those terms are good examples of some outsiders' mispronunciation of Appalachia, Lynn points out—but they mean a lot more than that. Would it be mercy killing (euthanasia) to put the "monsters" crawling from the mines out of their misery? Was Orpheus brave? He lacked trust the myth implies—but how much trust can one put in Hades?

There's more than enough blame here to go around. The speaker seems willing to take some on himself. His first job is as a receptionist at a pill-mill doctor's office. His second is at a law firm that defends coal companies. *Another day in the word mines,* the lawyers joke.

Wait, you might be thinking, this doesn't sound like poetry. It sounds like a novel or memoir, but there is no linear narrative. Much (though not all) of this book is composed of square prose blocks that work together like polyphony in music. For instance, one paragraph describing the extortion practiced by the fire department of ancient Rome (sell us your house cheap and we'll put this fire out) is followed by a paragraph in which the speaker watches helplessly as a good friend is seriously burned. Each of these segments is fresh and interesting in itself; each has an apparently different subject—yet they harmonize. To read this book requires constant parallel processing. *That* is what makes it poetry. What we might call motifs or "subject rhymes" are interwoven throughout. Fire is one. Prometheus (like Dante) makes an appearance. He famously steals fire from the gods and finds himself chained to the rock where, "the liver regenerates every morning the eagle keeps/eating keeps eating . . . with the patent for OxyContin set to run/out in 2013 Purdue Pharma reformulates it . . . no one steals from gods."

Perhaps the most salient fire story is the one based on the movie *Talladega Nights*, a film featuring NASCAR racing. Actor Will Farrell's character is afflicted with the illusion of "going up in flames" so that his buddy runs across the track yelling, *"Please don't/let the invisible fire hurt my friend."* This causes the speaker to laugh uproariously until he finds out that invisible fire, caused by burning methanol, *is* a problem in car racing. There *are* invisible fires and one could say that the so-called opiate crisis is one—one in which a friend and a friendship are in very real danger. Lynn tells a story by way of a series of digressions which turn out to be analogues of one another. The town pill mill, for instance, and the aforementioned Roman fire department are similarly extortionist, as are the coal mines that have left a patchwork of destruction in the region. These apparent digressions are so interesting that we forget to wonder if we've gone too far afield, and then, some word or image will tip us off and we can see again how the pieces fall together.

As for the Mothman, when I first saw the word I imagined it must refer to some superhero I'd never heard of, but no. It's an apparition first seen by teenagers near Point Pleasant, West Virginia, in the mid 1960s. They were frightened by what they described as a huge bird with red eyes that pursued them. (The rationally inclined speculated that it may have been a sandhill crane.) Subsequent sightings became vaguer but more dramatic: an ominous winged humanoid who appeared in the area of disasters. It came to be known as a harbinger. Lynn has chosen his avatar brilliantly. The apparition was always ambiguous (not to say nebulous) and never actually managed to give a meaningful warning—though a warning against the effects of oxycodone or strip mining might have been helpful. The Mothman persona in the poem is a naïve kid from a so-called flyover state who tries to find out who he is by googling himself. He learns he is a harbinger, but doesn't know what the word means. He also learns that most people don't believe he exists.

This book is a warning in itself. It warns us to look to our language. By the end, the speaker has joined a world where "every dollar/is complicit." He fears that, in the decade since the recounted events, he has "lost the difference between balm and *blame* pressed *complicit* into/*complacent*." Those words do slide together easily on the tongue. We are left to wonder if we've done the same.

This book not only deserves your attention, but will quickly grab it. It's a powerful and important debut.

RAE ARMANTROUT

Mothman
Apologia

(The Mothman Gets High)

.

Yes.   There is a point at which any person gets tired

of knowledge.   You could call this   a *threshold,*

or you could call this   *the point at which a person*

gets tired   of knowledge.   I'll tell you this:

I've never felt further   from another than when

standing beside them   trying to point out a star.

PART I

(The Mothman Googles Its Own Name)

The sleepless corners of the internet
call me a *harbinger*. A word I learned
how to say but not spell—like *syringe*,
like *tourniquet*—until after I'd already
begun to doubt my own existence. How
did I come to live life as a warning?
Same as you: disappointment strung out

together in series, the way August's
Christmas lights hang on to a mood.
Never off, never all the way on.
Scrolling pages of me asleep among
you, on t-shirts, tattoos. A red-eyed
bird, a migration without a name.
Ramps for off-route eighteen wheelers.

Jackknife as a form of crying. I'm older
than the selfie, not the self. This too
turned out to be a way of staying
invisible. I'm starting to get good at the
others. Don't you recognize my absence
from your rearview camera? I wonder if
the interstate ever follows itself home.

First of Ten Elegies for Fire and Oxycodone

In ancient Rome   fire departments worked like this   your house catches fire
someone shows up   with his own brigade of firemen   offers to buy
your house on the cheap   every second you wait   the price drops   every
second you remember   the price drops   every second you wonder   the price
drops   till you give in and sell   then   only then   do the firefighters go
to work   you wouldn't   couldn't   know it but your house   was gone
the moment it started burning   or at least the moment   the burning slipped
beyond your control   reduced to the question   of what you could get for it

—

I don't   can't   remember any of the details   of you catching fire   I know
it happened   because I saw the singed grass in the yard   I know because
your dad yelled   at the rest of us after   in a voice he only ever used for you
I know because   we drove you   to the hospital   every night for weeks
to get your wounds dressed   because the hospital tech   told you   told us
stories   about Narcan   about insurance fraud   about medical billing scams
as he unwrapped you   looked you over   the oxycodone wearing off
wrapped you up again   a gift opened   just long enough   to decide to give away

Second of Ten Elegies for Fire and Oxycodone

That fireman racket   they say   is how the first billionaire   got made
Rome's version of one anyway   Marcus Licinius Crassus   folks used to think
he's the shitbird   the word *crass* comes from   he ain't   we get it straight
from the Latin for *stout*   people don't think much   about him these days
you know   it's still the way   billionaires get made   just dress it up
in extra steps   no one notices   people are good   at not noticing
what they are paid   not to see   I believed in Santa   that stout impossibility
for years after finding   the stack of presents   under the tarp in the barn

—

Heard it took you a second   to notice the flames   noticed first   everyone else
their expressions   you mimicked the O   of their mouths   yours a dark hole
in a larger circle of fire   you dropped to the grass   started rolling   supposed
to do it back and forth   like a rolling pin   but you never had patience
for baking   you just rolled   rolled   rolled yourself   the whole way down
the hill   into the gravel road   half an acre away   something we had
to explain later   to the nurses   as they picked little rocks   from curdled skin
with tweezers   the way we used to sneak candies   from cookies at Christmas

(The Mothman at Twelve)

If it were love   then I would have known

where to put it   something I have   always

held gently   in that space   between my

eyebrows   the one shrinking   just a bit

while the rest of me   grows   one my sister

tells me   I'm gonna need   to pluck if

I ever expect   to be held   no one told me

what to do   with this or   what to do with

all their anger   so I hold it   the way fingers

clamp down against   a live wire   I still feel

the jolts   of the cow fence   impounding

my jaw   the wrath   I clench in these

shoulders   junk drawer of the body   waiting

for someone   to come back for it   I'm afraid

of them   how they get   whenever I lose

another thing   given to me   for safekeeping

Psalm for the Haters in the Back

As a child, I read once about
      a criminal on the run so long

she forgot her own name, forgot
      even that she was on the run at all;

no one more surprised by her
      capture in the end than herself.

It was the sort of thing I didn't
      believe was possible but

also the sort of thing I figured
      would probably happen to me.

Maybe it already has. Here I am
      not counting down the days until

the cops show up and kick these doors
      down in the name of someone else's law.

When that time comes, when the front door
      swings off its hinges, I hope I know what to do

like so many sea turtle hatchlings
      squirming towards an ocean,

a lost dog breaking into a run when it
      hears its name for the first time in years.

Voicemail from My Mother

for Claudia Emerson

You know, I haven't heard from you in a while. Did I tell you
        a bird flew into the house?
Found an open door on a cold day. Something small,

like a chickadee, but even more chickadee than that.
        I chased it around the house
with an upturned broom until I lost track through all that

sweeping of dirty air. This was a ways back, two cats ago.
        I didn't see it fly out,
so it's hung in my mind ever since. An unclosed parenthesis.

I've braced myself, the way the ear hears a squeal of brakes
        and begs for a thud.
Braced myself to find a tiny skeleton each time I clean

behind the curtains or rearrange the furniture. Today,
        opening the drawer
of cords that go to things I probably already threw away,

it flew out, perched briefly on my shoulder,
        then alighted hard
and I mean hard into the mirror of the closed window.

(The Mothman Pronounces Appalachia)

I say it *Appalachia* because there's a goddamn latch in it
and folks from far off rush in with a correction: *Appalayshia*

they say, as if there is something about the latch they are afraid of.
As if it needs to be dashed like the o in G-d. As if they're scared

that fiddling with it might knock a lid open and out of all these
mineshafts climb monsters, those of us they want to leave buried

under these hills. As if that hasn't already happened. What is strip
mining if not a way of tearing a lid off this whole place? That's not

a rhetorical question. How do you think I got out to begin with?
That's not one either. I am trying. I am trying to understand why

no one asks to understand mothpeople when all we wanted was
a warning. Still, assumptions fly in as far off as sandhill cranes.

Let me ask you what you think of us, the ones that climbed out
of some other Hades so long ago we waved to Orpheus on his way

inside. Once I dropped back down to gently put him out of his
impossible misery but when I told him where this drafty shaft leads

he corrected me *Appalayshia?* No it rhymes with *come back atcha*
the ways *Yeats* rhymes with *hates* not *heats*. *Appalachia* doesn't

rhyme with *euthanasia* any more than *Eurydice* rhymes with
cowardice and while I carry her back with me, we practice it

together: *Appalachia Appalachia*. Close that latch, turn the lock.
Like Yeats said about a poem, we click it shut like a box.

Third of Ten Elegies for Fire and Oxycodone

Fire fighting   an event   at the 1900 Olympics in Paris   sounds stupid
I know   but like so many stupid things   is true   the Americans win
the gold   Italians silver   the rest of the truth   only two teams competing
the sport never   part of the games again   still I count it as a win   forgive me
I'm old enough to know   the harm patriotism conceals   seen the photos
how they used to pledge the flag   arms straight out   a way we never will again
I know the way you'd brag   if you were here   *eat shit Italy*   *Crassus too*
ugly   a title we never lost   with you gone   a last thing to hold onto

—

Burned in my mind   what you said after   you stood up from the fire
about stop drop and roll   one of those grade school things   you never
think of   but comes back fast   the Pledge   the Macarena   riding a bike
though I tried that back   when I went off to college   ended up head over
handlebars   in the campus fountain   bricked my phone   I was afraid
too afraid to ask   my father for a new one   left it in rice for weeks
at first to cure it   then after a while   a way to keep imagining   each morning
it would start working again   that things would   could   go back as before

Fourth of Ten Elegies for Fire and Oxycodone

An American story   Arthur and Mortimer and Raymond Sackler   three brothers
all doctors   take that oath   start that company   pills put out the fires
that come with living   the doctors find   a problem   *addiction*
as businessmen   find the solution   *more*   of what they already sell
backfiring   that's what firefighters call it   when to fight a wild fire   they start
a gentle one   we learn this on the field trip   to the firehouse   have us dig
a fire line in the woods   to show us a controlled burn   their ax I drag ever slower
backfiring   when they teach you a thing until   you stop wanting to learn

—

The year I turned 14 you 13   wildfires set in Shenandoah   on Halloween
could be seen from space   and smelled from both our backyards   the one set
by accident   unattended campfire   soon swallowed   the one set on purpose
some shitbirds   smoking something   in a fire tower   the kind of bad idea
we didn't yet have   by the time you got your license   Skyline Drive had got
reduced to moonscape   I remember winding through the park   in your sister's
Dodge Dakota   past forests wearing char like a costume   then wildflowers
how a mouse problem   becomes a snake problem   if you let it go long enough

(The Mothman at the Psychiatrist's Office in the City)

It is a good idea not to be traumatized by fire
because if you're looking for it you'll find it
everywhere even the engine of your car even
beneath the stovetop sleeping quietly even
the shirt pocket of your friend who also keeps
it on the tip of his tongue and in a candle
on the corner of the bar it is a good idea not
to be traumatized by fire because if you are
alone with it you become alone with its
thoughts and hoo boy let me tell you fire
thinks some real awful awful awful
it is a good idea not to be traumatized by fire
because there are whole parts of West
Virginia named after explosives which is
where they saw the first of us mothpeople
and yes it is a good idea not to be traumatized
by fire because if you fixate on it you can't
rule out the possibility of summoning it with
the pale force of your fear it is a good idea
not to be traumatized by fire because it is a
good idea not to be traumatized because it is
fire not an idea to be traumatized by but fire
actual fire I'm telling or I'm trying to tell you
I'm not afraid of the idea but the thing itself

It Was Time Again for Bushhogging the Paddock

and there I was five-foot-four and most way old enough
to drive and so with the kind of deliberation useful
for disguising fear my father went about showing me
the stick shift on the old Ford tractor the one he bought
with his first government wages and loved so much
he even had it loaded on a lowboy and brought down
to this house when he moved off the mountain this house
where every morning he took coffee on the porch
watching two wild turkeys disappear into the woods
with the last of the dark and on this day he taught me how
the clutch engages and to keep careful on the revolutions
per minute leaving one hand on the wheel the other
steady behind me on the mower lever ready to cut it
at his hand signal and this day was a turning over of something
like an engine coughing slowly while my father walked ahead
scouting in that grass so tall only the shoulders of his blue
shirt pecked out above the green-brown stalks that my machine
trampled and spat out behind me with the constant turning
of that heavy steel blade he explained was dull by design to whack
but not catch in the dense growth and here I was cutting clean
the swath behind me in the field scanning to my side to check
for big rocks and other unmowables and I might as well have
been Hannibal riding an elephant over an alp and I felt the earth
yielding for the first time to my adultness as I sawed a slow
zigzag back across the paddock but then it was there the flutter
of wings alongside me and my father yelling which seen from
a tractor is all visual a mouth opening all the way and not
closing overwhelmed by the din of the engine his hands
waved a gesture what gesture the signal and we watched
two turkeys flee to the woods while we waited for the blade
to sputter stopped and there in the earned silence I climbed
down from the giant stilled tire and my father pointed me
to the dashed nest the dozen broken eggs and whatever
he'd yelled he'd already gotten it all out and now was well

past speaking he simply turned and walked the long way back
up to the house through the tall grass that closed behind
him in the buzzing air and so I followed hoping we might
both disappear and so we leave the tractor where it stops
and no one finishes mowing the paddock this year
or the next or even the one after that which is to say
this is how a field returns itself to woods.

Prayer for the Shitstains

Other teams called us the Cow Crappers because they
couldn't call us the Shitstains in public. All of them,
from the town teams on down to the trailer park team,
called us the Cow Crappers because we practiced in

the coach's cow pasture where every kid who complained
about the wet hops that grounders took off of fresh patties
ran laps until he knew better, ran laps until he could field
a dirty thing cleanly: plant your feet a shoulder-width apart,

glove all the way to the dirt like your arm is just the latest
thing the earth has sprouted. Bend your body, boy, to knock
down anything your glove can't catch. Don't act like you've
never been hit before. Don't you dare look away or even

wince as the ball pops off a rock or rooster-tails through the
manure piles. Coach can tell that you chickened out by the way
the shit flecks your ear instead of your nose. He says the
bruises on your chest heal faster than the ones on your pride.

My father was the first base coach. I would later learn how
he'd put the third base coach in jail for spousal abuse
many years before, the kind of thing no one mentioned,
the kind of thing you learn not to talk about like the wet hops,

like the bruises, like the shit that stayed on the ball long after
the play was over, a thing that stained your fingers green.
This is how we learned manure is made out of grass, water
and time but mostly grass. How it helps the new grass grow.

That's the thing about manure: it helps things grow.
You can call us what you will but we are gonna make
the grass grow. Just watch. Come see the only trick
I ever learned: how to field a dirty thing clean.

(The Mothman Watches a TV Movie and Resolves to Steal the Declaration of Independence)

Does it have to be true, that everything

we touch, we break a little? Josh's garden fence.

My bicycle. Reva's walk to work after you

shouted her name. Can you give me something

of a counterexample? I ran out yesterday—

the TV showed pictures of labs in California

so sterile breathing was its own kind

of crime. We always thought of ourselves

as too small to smudge anything, yet by design

or indifference, our flashes bleached even

the founding parchments. No one knows

what they will do with power until they have it.

None of us believes we got it when they do.

I Never Knew What They Meant
by Flyover Country

until the first time someone put me on a plane, windowed me
into the congregation looking down on our fields stretched out
endless in orderly blanks, redactions in the transcripts of the trial
of man versus nature. All this holy squinting at scrimshaw country
roads draped with power lines—trip wires lying in wait for the giants
we just sort of mice around. I watched the others look down on
our Fridays racing Opal Road to hit the tiny hill that drops stomachs
like a roller coaster, headlights off for cops. Eighty. Ninety. Ninety-five
in a fifty-five, how Kyle's brother talked about defusing IEDs on tour—
snip whichever wire you want, you'll only find out if you're a hero.
We learned a word for this, it's *reckless* in court, *predestination*
in church. Funny how a thing gets a different name there. *Robe* becomes
vestment. Bench becomes *pew. Truth* grows a capital letter. *Anything
to help believe*, Mom says, though when it comes to theology we are
Presbyterian in casseroles only. *This is the word of God*, says the pastor
into the microphone. *See you at the picnic after. See you at the finish*,
says Kyle's Honda Civic. *See you never* says his brother's IED.

The Best Shot in the House

According to my mother, fresh shell casings are warm
    with the sadness of separation.
She was never specific about whose. The only other thing
         she ever said about guns was
Where's the fun in point-and-pull? So I resolved to find it

for the same reasons I insisted on eating baker's chocolate
    with a straight face, for the
same reason as a teenager she smoked her way through
         the whole pack of punishment
cigarettes, then coughing, asked my grandfather for another.

This is how it came to pass that the first time my father
    took me shooting, I amused myself
catching spent casings as they fell until my fingers blistered
         around the brass. Later, tending
the burns, she said *I don't see the point in point-and-pull.*

There was no use talking back because it was understood
    that she was the best shot
in the house, just something, I was told, girls learn better
         in West Virginia. I never saw her
fire a real gun. The only proof deposed by video games:

with each click of the orange pistol, the Duck Hunt ducks
    would fall and she would take
another step back until she ran out of room or cord.
         She never played for long.
It's just point-and-pull and where's the fun in that?

By then she'd be against the wall, standing on the living
    room couch, cord so taut
that when she'd drop the toy weapon it would spring
         from her hand like something
hot with the disappointment of the sudden separation.

PART II

(The Mothman Leaves the Used Car Lot Empty-Handed)

You said the problem with driving a pickup is
never getting to be the one riding in the bed.

This is what I meant when I told you I had
trouble choosing grace. I want to, I do.

But also I need to be one of the ones who
gets to lie back against the wheel well.

To let the breeze lick my face, let it trick
the eyes into crying, let it raise my hair

like a drink before a toast—the one moment
I can still be sure all speech is blessing.

The Season We Danced Alone While Pumping Gas

Virginia, October 2002

Recall the crappy metronome fear made out of the gulps
        of the fuel pump. The sniper the news
conjured behind every parked car between here & Baltimore.

Nobody expecting to outdance the bullet—just relying
        on that old hiking joke: *a slow*
enough companion & you don't have to outrun the bear.

Every head bob, contagious. Every shimmy from the customer
        at the next pump, a challenge we were
compelled to accept. This is a dance-off now because I refuse

to let someone else's ducks & sways make my body the path
        of least resistance, to let a bullet close
the circuit our parents had opened just sixteen years before.

The season we danced alone while pumping gas you stopped
        shrugging off the crosshairs: you'd read
that when you put bugs in a jar & shake it, they fight each other

instead of the thing that shakes them. Let us fight the things
        that shake us, you said. You said
if there is someone pointing a gun at us & let's be clear

there is nobody—statistically nobody—pointing a gun at us
        but if there is, are you going to tell them
where to point it? To let your body beg *shoot them not me?*

The season we danced alone while pumping gas, our homecoming
        game was played away. Its dance, perhaps
redundant, cancelled altogether. Ten people died before month-end.

That season, I was still ironing every task of driving into habit
        so even now I find myself sashaying
to the pump before I slide the nozzle in & pull the trigger.

Walking Blues Not Packaged for Individual Sale

I learned the word *bodega*
     the same day I learned *arbitrage*
riding with you down to Richmond
     to buy armloads of the cheap cigarettes,
the ones you'd pack duffled
     aboard a Chinatown bus to resell on the sly
in Brooklyn. Back on Earth,
     driving your truck home alone, I turned
both words over in my mouth
     again and again, polishing the gemstones.
My mother learned *bodega* from
     "Diamonds on the Soles of Her Shoes"
and asked me to take a picture
     of the first one I saw when I visited you.
When I tried, you told me *Don't preserve*
     the evidence, dumbshit so I never got one.
Besides, whatever glitter Paul Simon
     burnished onto the word had gotten lost
among the toilet paper rolls and
     rubber gloves that lined the ceilings,
though I found a glimmer of it
     napping on the warmth of the ATM, a cat
who was named Lucy not after diamonds
     but after the cigarettes. This was back before
you figured out how much more
     you can make by just stealing what you wanted.
Back when I still thought of myself
     as the kind of friend who would visit you in jail.

(The Mothman Picks Up a Misdemeanor)

The worst true story is all valley towns
look the same. The same Wendy's, the same
turn lanes, the same Days Inns lining
the same divided highways blooming
the same out of Main Streets like lichen.

This town was the same and I would fight
anybody—*any body*—that said so. Put teeth
through an elbow. I was here to spit blood in
a drive-thru cup. I was here and who was I?
Who was I to be a vision of anyplace else?

Fifth of Ten Elegies for Fire and Oxycodone

Heard this one   2010 Obion County Tennessee   guy forgets to pay his $75
per month fire fee   his house ablaze   he calls up   the fire department
they answer but don't   won't   come   he's not on the list   for this kind
of salvation   he begs   he begs   it's only when   his neighbors' house
catches too that they bother   to come out   even then   keep their hoses
spraying   on the other side of   the fence   put out half the fire   wait around
putting it out again   each time   it jumps the fence   his house still burning
guy loses   everything   ain't that   the most American thing you ever heard

—

How much after discharge do you remember   being outpatient   all those
weeks we would   drive once a day to get your   burns re-dressed   the most
time I'd spent with you   in years   the most   I ever would again do you
remember what we talked about   because I don't   just how earnest   your
presence had suddenly become   your gentleness   and my surprise at its
return   you called out to deer grazing   on the other side   of a fence   as they
blurred by   gave them names   one by one of neighbors   I had forgotten
pain pills kept   you pretty loopy   I could hear your teeth as   they wore off

Sixth of Ten Elegies for Fire and Oxycodone

The Greek myth goes like this   you probably know it   but I had to look it up
Prometheus   steals fire   from Zeus and the other gods   gives it to humans
heaven's prowess now mortal   Zeus sticks it to Prometheus   cause he knows
knowledge   knows how sharp its edge can be   chains him to a rock   an eagle
eating his liver all day   the liver regenerates every morning   the eagle keeps
eating   keeps eating   keeps eating   with the patent for OxyContin   set to run
out in 2013   Purdue Pharma reformulates it   gets a new patent   lobbies the old
drug illegal   no one steals from gods   no one dulls the blade of knowledge

—

That summer   my first desk job   insurance intakes   at a doctor's office
the relief of air conditioning   pharma reps catering our lunches   released from
the fear   of dropping a ladder on a foreman   of threading my thumbnail
with another drill bit   the good doc scheduled   in five minute increments
I retyped patient addresses   all hill towns sixty miles off   the waiting room
so full and grumpy   I wondered about the etymology of *patient*   but never what
makes a person   drive hours through the mountains   wait hours for a flicker
with the doc   I was not paid to wonder   I quit before I ever typed your name

(The Mothman Dabbles in Etymology)

You should know I was not the first

to think the word *forgive* implied an

exchange, a deal. Bags, bills, palms.

After all it means, at its root, *to give*

completely. Or in some translations,

to abandon, as in a debt or grief.

With this knowledge, I entered

the world determined to prove   that

giving and *abandonment* were the

same thing. All my life and now

to discover they just looked alike

as the shadows cast by mercy.

Coming To

in this stutter of light, that static of neurons whimpering like dogs

on the Fourth. A voice—though I didn't, even couldn't, know

what a voice was. Or attach it to a body, a person, a patience holding

my head up out of this mud. These banks, some lake. The never

of going back. Water moving faster without getting closer. Strange ache,

a sun-shower. I was surprised everything had a character: either more

fear or less. Bridges connecting to clouds. Religious. The mouse I named

so someone would stop asking me to kill it. Someone else's car askew.

The first full thought I wrangled into form was *I better tell her*

I'm okay. This thought—how I discovered that I was.

I Remember You Best as the Man

asleep on my chest, warm breath somehow
the exact opposite of sex. How I came

to know you take your tea with honey
if I got any. Sugar? Then nothing. It's true

we teach each other how we want
to be held. You brimming hot—another mug

I had to shuffle-step up a narrow stair. Once
right after waking and always again, but decaf

before turning in. Because loving you
was another impossibility, who was I

to notice when it happened? When it did
it bloomed in me, milk in the steeping dark.

(The Mothman Might Oughta Go Home)

I say *might oughta* because *oughta*
knows it's not nice enough on its own.
I say *double modal* so nobody leaves here
calling me names. I name nothing, exactly
how much Mothpeople can say. I say
language is a trap time set to catch its own
damn self—a trap time set then forgot
to check. Language is a place trapped
in time and you may should watch your
mouth when you speak. A no-kill trap is
the most humane up until everyone forgets
about it. Everyone but the one it caught.

Augury

I wasn't afraid of water until I began
to carry this phone all the time,
like my grandfather did the secret
revealed at his funeral. Best time
to meet you is just after the storm
stops, the beaches still empty
as woodstoves in August—
before anyone's thought to squint
at puddles out the window to ask
if the rain has given up. Whenever
it's like this a kestrel shelters
on what's left of my windowsill.
Wet feathers look so much like
your hair coming fresh off a swim.
In the receiving line a stranger
in a walker held my hand and cried
how she loved him. *We had many*
late nights, though I shouldn't talk.
But she couldn't stop herself—who can?—
so she repeated it again and again
until discretion was only a boutonniere
on the dead. I tried not to look
at my grandmother, sobbing perhaps
for a different reason. As a child, I loved
to take refuge from a downpour in the deep
end of the pool. Practiced hiding
from something by immersing myself in it.
I shouldn't talk. The Romans watched
birds to understand the future
though now we do it just because
we like it, the way morning's
discretion retreats from the past.

About the Phones

Closing my car door, you always say   *Watch*
for deer and text when you get home.
I want to, I do, but I will forget.
Time moves and I forget.   Look
I am trying, I am, but it's not the kind
of thing that trying solves.

Once
on the side of a highway, a cop told me
about dragging a full grown buck out
the windshield of a wrecked car all by himself.
About the sounds it made, *Like the devil learning*
what regret feels like. About the woman it kicked
to death in the driver's seat. The phone call
he had to make to her grown daughter after
whose first question was, *Did the deer survive?*

Different cop, different time, different highway.
Said she keeps her phone on silent then spoke
about securing the crime scene in that classroom
in Blacksburg where the one student shot
all the others. Every single one of them
had a cell phone, she said, and for hours after
every single one rang and rang or vibrated
across the floor in the same slow way
that blood pools. No one was allowed to answer,
no one, so instead the phones rang all night
until batteries were empty, voicemails full
of a thousand *Call me when you get this so I know*
you're okays. Turns out time moves the way
blood does. Batteries too. Runs out
like a startled deer across a road.   Listen
I am trying to find a way to tell you this.
There are things that trying solves but this
is not one of them.

PART III

(The Mothman on the
Bullshit Curse of Interesting Times)

Shit yeah, when I was younger I wished for awful things
to happen. I thought living was interesting and only knew

interesting as awful. I saw cars as concealed chases,
Chekov's gun permit. I coagulated across state lines.

That's how time went, awful quick. As awful as quick.
In jail Elijah wrote letters just to get letters back, just

to have something to pad under his flimsy mattress.
I bought the softest paper in the store and then forgot

to write. Everything I learned, I wished I hadn't. Nothing:
the only thing I'm glad to know. I take the long way home:

anything not to smell the long barns of the chicken farm.
Every morning I pray: no blood, no feathers in my eggs.

Breakfast awful early to remember cages. Now I only wish
for better sleep. Me and Eli trying awful hard to nod off.

Seventh of Ten Elegies for Fire and Oxycodone

Larry Levis   living down   in the flat part of Virginia   draws his life
In a Late Style of Fire   his obituary doesn't say it   but drugs killed him one
way or another   of course they don't print   those sorts of things   in
papers   didn't used to in poems neither   where he wrote about jacking off
sending meth for god to try   he was teaching then   at the same college
we'd find you   or you'd find yourself   getting kicked out of   for growing
weed   I wonder what Levis knew   about Rome   its firemen   the most
American things   you ever heard of   that never heard of   America

—

When that great aunt died   we included   *After a long battle with breast cancer*
in the draft of her obituary   the paper took out breast   too sexy for the news
when you died   nobody included how in the paper   for the sake of decorum
as if they were pulling something off   as if people around here   saw an obit
for a 25-year-old   no listed cause of death   thought anything other than
overdose   or suicide   the only folks fooled   are those from the future
the ones combing death records   to find out how we lived   the trouble with
decorum   the future won't know   who did this to us   who and how bad

Eighth of Ten Elegies for Fire and Oxycodone

The only literature class I ever take   that first year in college   makes us read
all 34 cantos   of Dante's *Inferno*   that guy sure thinks a lot   about fire
sure talks a lot of shit   Dante is Italian   sure he knows   all about Crassus
I can talk as much   shit as I want   as a matter of law   you can't defame
the dead   his book is pretty grim   I make it only part-way   look up
the rest online   I'm not a bad student   but I mean   it's a very long
poem   the gist   of the gist   of the gist of it   in case you don't
have the time   the poet invents hell   puts all his enemies   in there by name

—

Charon in the driver's seat   of my truck   only I didn't know   what Charon
looked like   so it was you   in the driver's seat   but I knew in dreams
you're Charon   ferryman of the afterlife   the good doc rode shotgun
Crassus in the truck bed   chauffeured as billionaires do   could hear his teeth
now that the oxy faded   Arthur   and Mortimer   and Raymond Sackler
with him in the back   shitbirds   you could hear their teeth   you could hear
all their teeth   and no painkillers   from here on out   it just keeps
going   Prometheus and his eagle   this one long road over the mountains

(The Mothman Startles the Neighbors)

After moving out here from some real
big where, the new neighbors piled
bags of garbage at the end of their
long gravel drive, *waiting waiting
waiting* to be collected by the gloves
of some city that didn't and wouldn't exist.

First, raccoons. Then bears, scattering
used napkins all over my woods. Birds
stole drawstrings, plastic straws. But trash
trucks? None. I worry, have I held out
this way for love's faulty assumptions?
All these pink nests I've found in the trees.

Extraction

Another day in the word mines, they joked
at the law firm for coal companies the summer
the old senator died and even the President
brought his sadness to West Virginia. That night,
I worked so late I got trapped in his secure perimeter
till the motorcade disappeared into a helicopter.
With nowhere to go, I paced up and down the empty
river in front of the glass building where a Pontiac
car show stretched along Kanawha Blvd. It was so hot
only ghosts bothered coming. Dead show, dead
company, dead town. This is where I stood
on the levee and watched the barges pass like anthracite
to graphite. I came back to an email from my boss
who said everybody with an office window was sure
I was about to jump. *What an image you made against
the water in your Goodwill suit.* I didn't know this
was a joke. I had four hundred dollars in the bank, sixty thousand
in debt and a room in my grandmother's attic. Broke, a city
I was passing through like smog. The next day I left
work early, drove forty minutes halfway to Beckley.
The Alleghenies cradling the toll road, same as I
remembered. Sneaking into the Kayford Mine, I climbed
the mountain—what was left of it. Trees gave way
to moonscape so I turned
around surrounded by the wrong
sides of the ridges' facades. I hadn't counted on the dust.
What an image I must've made against the bald earth.
My suit spattered past saving. The dry cleaning, even here,
thirty bucks a week. In the glass building, they joked
Coal, it keeps the lights on, then looked inside and laughed.

The Summer After the Winter
I Taught You How to Start a Fire

You asked me what I knew about thermals—
heat's tendency to rise, cool, fall again and so
I showed you how to recognize the circle
of turkey vultures over our neighbor's field
as a clue another calf had died. Immediately
you declared yourself the Detective of All Dead
Things. *Something's dead*, you'd say, squinting
skyward. *Case closed. That'll be fifty dollars.*
It was one of your better jokes and as with all jokes
funny at first then a little less until repeated only
as an epitaph for how funny it once was.
Fifty American dollars. This debt smoldering
like your anger after I told you the words
I love you work the same way. I was careful
to say so in the joking tone reserved
for the parts of this living too disappointing
to speak plain. *Something's dead*, you'd say,
a skill precisely too late to be of any use.
Same as me here explaining the joke, the check
I'd mail if I had your new address.

(The Mothman Reads from *The Book of the Dead*)

Heading west to Charleston again, every dollar is complicit. Harrisonburg wafting chickenshit even from the interstate, Covington those rotting eggs three days a week. Fayette County like the dusty ghosts on Rukeyser's lists when she wrote *I first discovered what was killing these men*. She was not the first to discover what was killing them. Thing is those empowered to discover it weren't interested in what knowledge could save. I grew up believing John Henry was a West Virginia kind of hero because he won the race and lost his life. I know now John Henry is a West Virginia hero because he's a warning that your bosses will kill you. When they closed another tunnel outside Charleston they draped a flag across its mouth. Quiet. Every tunnel can shout more names of the dead. Every tunnel in this state is a warning. Every mineshaft. Every hole in an arm. Listen. Mothpeople are warnings—ways of naming a certain kind of hero. A warning is just a hero that asks you to save yourself somehow. Most times, it doesn't work. Too bad everything is extractable with enough cash and disregard. I wanna hear West Virginia as something other than muffled warnings. Here, this catalogue of our joy.

Ninth of Ten Elegies for Fire and Oxycodone

That dumb joke   in *Talladega Nights*   Will Ferrell's delusion of going up
in flames   John C. Reilly wails   as he runs across the racetrack   *Please don't*
let the invisible fire hurt my friend   I laughed hard enough   to soak out any
flame imagine then   my embarrassment at finding invisible fire is an actual
problem in car racing   fuel called methanol   burns colorless   doesn't even
smoke   all sorts of videos   up on the internet   the Indy 500   pit crews
writhing from unseeable flames turns out you can run around burning   nobody
notices   wave your arms   roll around   still no one believes you're on fire

—

I watched the DVD   with your sister once   after the accident   that scene
the stop drop and roll she threw up in her mouth   in a sudden way as if a pipe
inside her burst   oh her face   as it dribbled down her chin   I snapped
the disc   like a communion cracker   when I picture your face   I see your
stippled freckles   giving way   to the fractal coastline   of your burns
a topographic map   some far off country   we could never afford to visit
imagine you there   making the local dishes   burnt tinfoil   shoplifted
shoelaces   Narcan left like cookies for Santa   roses in little glass tubes

Tenth of Ten Elegies for Fire and Oxycodone

The law of causation   has a special doctrine   *the two fires rule*   preserves
responsibility for damage done   by multiple causes   each sufficient to cause
the whole harm   say two guys start   two different fires   in the same woods
behind your house   they meet as fires do   shake hands   join forces
swallow your home   when called to court   each arsonist paints the other
as the whole damn cause   attests to his own absolution   since if he didn't start
his fire   your house would still be gone   a logic hard to argue with   under the
old rules   say three brothers start a company   in the woods behind your life

—

Fire has always   raged or smoldered   same verbs   given to anger   the way
you were   remember the time before   it burned hidden in you   a pilot light
before our skinny wrists   climbed their way   out of locker room trash cans
before you smashed your saxophone   to spite that dickhole   of a band teacher
before they showed us any other way   to prove a point   before your grow arrest
before your fire fall   before spoons went missing   from your parents' kitchen
before all that   I remember you   taking apart a lighter   just to understand it
how you'd put it all   back together again   your delight   when it still burned

(The Mothman Drops Out)

When we started, when you started here
with me, we had such hopes. Such uses
for logic. Like gulps of air. Like body parts
and places to put them. I escaped from you
like a reason. Like bone does from a fossil.
I ached to become a ghost and when I did
I even ghosted the long pauses. Hush hush.
I wrote silence down instead of speaking it.
I write silence and the silence answers
with more silence. I write inhales. I write
the pauses and then haunt them too, until
they stay quiet and afraid in their corners.
Pause, I write. And pause silences pause.

Peepers in February

It helps to think of longing as a fever
the body uses to rid itself of lonely.
Sounds nice and like most nice things is wrong.
    The guy at the liquor store says my license
    expired so the computer won't let him
    sell me nothing. That's okay I'm already drunk
    on the government's fear I'm getting younger.
Sounds nice. Could make that a fairy tale if I tell it right.
    It's not like I even wanted the wine, just
    to show up at a friend's door with something
    to quibble over. I've been trying to write
    an elegy for candy bought for use
    of a gas station bathroom, eaten anyway.
Sounds nice but never seems to take. This year
    the crocuses popped up early, looked around
    for the sun as if trying to ask about a wrong
    left turn at Albuquerque. My friend, so happy
    to see them, was told twelve months ago
    she'd be dead inside of six. Turned waiting
    into a cause, at least a trip to the liquor store.
Sounds nice but you know I'm no good at renewing
    goodbyes, can't even get myself to the DMV.
    I stay home with the dusk chorus longing
    from the edge of the woods. I call you
    on the phone so you can hear them.
Sounds nice, right? Even if you don't know what they are.
    I've come to know that looking up
    spring peepers turns them back into frogs.
    A fairy tale so long as you run it in reverse.

Sneaking onto the Reservoir Again

Everything this year gave me it took back
quicker—lovers, money, reckless smiles
of restless friends. According to the awful math
of planets, summer's next. I brace for autumn
to come for it the way I used to collect you
drunk at a bar. If a season wants to stay—
to linger past enunciation like you were given to
so often—why stop it? What will October make
of its belligerence? Superheroes begging parents
to let them outside without jackets, you and I sweating
clean from the past? August is still here but you're not
so this time I paddle out alone, rowing the rare thing
easier without you. By sundown the water is warmer
than the air breezing over it. It radiates like a man
next to me in bed and I stretch my arms across it
out of instinct. The ranger's truck in a far field
cranking doo-wop because he thinks he's alone.
I stroke slow to the backbeat, harmonies splitting
and rejoining as they're carried to me over the water.
If they were birds we'd call that murmuration, fish
we'd call it schooling. If they were you, I'd know
that what we call the bad year has finally let go.

(The Mothman Looks Back)

Funny, I never knew when or where

the anger went, how we wouldn't miss it.

Years on, fires smoking in our backyards

or the backrooms of the bars our hairlines

disappear to: we all talk shit on the lovesick

ages—the music, that smolder, our tongues

on good parts of worse people. Yet no one

speaks of the rage, as if there is nobody

to remember it except you, the one too dead

to be bothered to show. Still, it's you I miss

Never those days before I knew grace

was a fire. An apology. Another thing

I could give away without having any less.

Let the Child Think She's Found an Arrowhead

As lies go, I know it is a weak one,
but since I am going to make her
walk this tractor-torn landscape
        either way,

I might as well leave her the patience
to keep her head down, her eyes treating each
rock in the churned earth like the answer
        to a question.

I know children can be easily discouraged, but
in the winter I have seen sparrows scan the
spent seed shells the same way after I forget
        to refill the feeder.

A Pangram for the Post-Modern Typefaces

Because the schoolchildren
who worshiped dinosaurs and gazed wide-eyed
into that night sky

became quantum physicists
and spent whole lifetimes proving exactly how
much we can't know

the rest of this poem
shrugged itself from the page and slid carefully
into the flowerbeds

leaving jettisoned
black cocoons barely clinging to the white
paper pulp.

Eleventh of Ten Elegies for Fire and Oxycodone

It's late last spring   maybe the last late spring   the sun not up   but getting there
a man walks   into Prospect Park the way   a house in a storm walks
into a lake   he lies down in its dewy   grass where   he lays an envelope
beside him   how I came to   remember the difference   between *lay*
and *lie*   *flee* and *fly* like   *burn* and *blight* he carries dirt   along to
spread   all around him   as fire line that thing I never learned   he's so
careful his flames won't   go beyond him *I apologize to you for this*   *mess*
he leaves a note leaves   a warning   fire as the metaphor   we shape   it

—

my friend who saw this   walking her dog told me guilty she mistook   his
burning for the sun going   up through the trees   every day I biked   past
the charred circle on my way   to work   remembering the man   never his
message   how I remember you   a decade gone never your   fear the way
I lost the difference   between *balm*   and *blame* pressed   *complicit* into
complacent   I learned to ditch a place like   an accent like this city
you never saw   where even the grass grew back   forgot that man   how you
were the first to tell me   the mind remembers joy as joy pain only as a concept

(The Mothman Gets Clean)

Yes.   Or when a person gets tired of trying

you could point to this point, you could call this

a knowledge.   Standing beside them, you will call

this *a tell.*   I have never tired of knowledge which

gets at the point: out there is a threshold at which

I felt further from another person   than any star.

Notes

Versions of certain poems printed in this volume have appeared in the following publications:

The Adroit Journal: "Augury"

American Literary Review: "Psalm for the Haters in the Back"

The Common: "Peepers in February"

Greensboro Review: "Voicemail from My Mother"

Infinite Rust: "Let the Child Think She's Found an Arrowhead"

Kestrel: "The Best Shot in the House" and "(The Mothman Pronounces Appalachia)"

Narrative: "It Was Time Again for Bushhogging the Paddock"

Sugar House Review: "A Pangram for the Post-Modern Typefaces"

Superstition Review: "The Season We Danced Alone While Pumping Gas"

Tampa Review: "Prayer for the Shitstains"

A cryptid of West Virginia folklore, the Mothman is said to be a human-size winged creature with glowing red eyes who appears as a warning before disasters, most notably the collapse of the Silver Bridge in Point Pleasant, West Virginia, in 1967.

"Voicemail from My Mother" draws on Claudia Emerson's poems "Metaphor" and "A Bird in the House" from her 2005 collection *Late Wife.*

"(The Mothman Pronounces Appalachia)" adapts a line from William Butler Yeats's letter to Dorothy Wellesley of September 8, 1935: "[A] poem comes right with a click like a closing box."

"Seventh of Ten Elegies for Fire and Oxycodone" incorporates images from the work of the poet Larry Levis, specifically the poems "My Story in a Late Style of Fire" and "God Is Always Seventeen."

"(The Mothman Reads from *The Book of the Dead*)" includes a line from Muriel Rukeyser's long documentary poem "The Book of the Dead," first published in 1938 about the Hawk's Nest Tunnel disaster in Fayette County, West Virginia, in which over 400 workers—mostly African-American—were killed by avoidable toxic drilling conditions. The line used is from the section "Absalom," which is written in persona.

"(The Mothman Reads from *The Book of the Dead*)" also includes references to the traditional folk song "John Henry," about a folk hero drilling the Big Bend Tunnel in Summers County, West Virginia.

"Ninth of Ten Elegies for Fire and Oxycodone" includes a line from *Talladega Nights: The Ballad of Ricky Bobby*, a 2006 feature film written by Will Ferrell and Adam McKay.

"Peepers in February" includes a catchphrase often used by the Warner Bros. cartoon character Bugs Bunny.

"A Pangram for the Post-Modern Typefaces" constitutes a pangram, which is a short passage containing all the letters of a language (e.g., "the quick brown fox jumps over the lazy dog"), traditionally used to demonstrate typewriters or fonts.

"Eleventh of Ten Elegies for Fire and Oxycodone" includes a reference to David Buckel, an accomplished and committed human rights lawyer who self-immolated in Prospect Park in Brooklyn, New York, in April 2018 as a warning against the dangers of fossil fuel dependency. May he rest in peace.

"(The Mothman Gets Clean)" is a rearranged version of the opening poem, "(The Mothman Gets High)."

As alluded to in the Elegies for Fire and Oxycodone, the Sackler brothers and their company, Purdue Pharma, are known for profiting off their well-documented practices that exacerbated, if not created, the opioid epidemic in the United States. According to the Centers for Disease Control, the opioid epidemic kills approximately 130 people every day in the United States. For further reading on the subject, see Patrick Radden Keefe's *Empire of Pain* (2021, Doubleday).

The advance and any royalities from this book received by the author have been and will be donated to families of those affected by the opioid epidemic and harm reduction organizations operating in Virginia and West Virginia.

Acknowledgments

Deep gratitude to Rae Armantrout and the readers of the Yale Series of Younger Poets Prize for believing in the Mothman, at least within these pages, and bringing this book into the world. I am indebted to Jennifer Banks, Jeff Schier, Ash Lago, and the incredible staff of Yale University Press for their patience and care with this text. Thank you Roger May for your beautiful photograph on the cover. I am forever grateful for the instruction of the late Claudia Emerson, my first poetry mentor, and the teachers that followed her—Catherine Barnett, Tina Chang, Major Jackson, Yusef Komunyakaa, Deborah Landau, Sally Wen Mao, Sharon Olds, and Ron Villanueva, among many others. Thank you Evelyn Madden, who believed in my writing before anybody else did, and Joseph DiBella and Carole Garmon, who taught me about writing without teaching writing. Thank you Steve Scafidi, who doesn't know me but whose poems showed me these woods are worthy of art. Thank you Alex Dimitrov, who asked me what I was afraid of and never stopped asking until I wasn't anymore. I am so thankful for my family and friends, from both Virginias to New York and beyond, who have kept me going in large and small ways they can't know. Special thanks to my parents and to Michael, Rick, and Wendy for your thoughtfulness and storytelling. Thank you Ann-Bailey, Peter, Harper, Lilly Bell, Will, and Olivia. Thank you Rose Bergdoll, Alex Campbell, Nathalie Chouery, Lyuba Docheva, Malik Fakiri, Marisa Falcon, Andrew Hamm, Victor Malaret, Kate McCormack, and my friends in Brooklyn. Thank you Stone Ferrell, Luke McCleary, Kyle Schuster, Molly Sheldon, and everyone from Mary Washington. Thank you Casey Jay Andrews, Roberto Castillo, Suzy Kopf, Michael Martelo, and Chris Reilly. Dearest thanks to all my friends at NYU who read drafts of poems in this book and handled them and me with care—Waleed Bhatti, Sasha Burshteyn, Sena Cebeci, Marissa Davis, Sara Elkamel, Bernard Ferguson, Harris Hayman, Nancy Huang, Jenna Lanzaro, Hannah Matheson, Hannah Seidlitz, Janelle Tan, and many others. And thank you Amanda Larson, for all of it, through all of it.